ESTATE   PUB

HASTINGS
BEXHILL

RYE   BATTLE   WINCHELSEA

G000141618

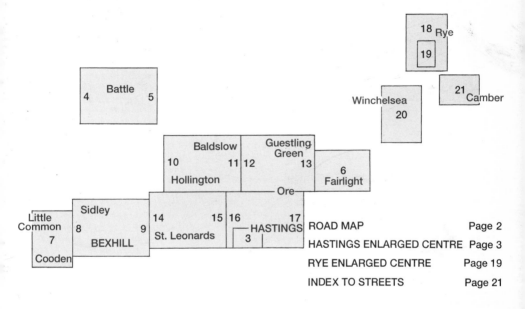

ROAD MAP	Page 2
HASTINGS ENLARGED CENTRE	Page 3
RYE ENLARGED CENTRE	Page 19
INDEX TO STREETS	Page 21

Every effort has been made to verify the accuracy of information in this book but the publishers cannot accept responsibility for expense or loss caused by any error or omission. Information that will be of assistance to the user of the maps will be welcomed.

The representation of a road, track or footpath on the maps in this atlas is no evidence of the existence of a right of way.

One-way Street	←
Car Park	P
Place of Worship	+
Post Office	●
Public Convenience	C
Pedestrianized	▨

Scale of street plans: 4 inches to 1 mile
Unless otherwise stated

Street plans prepared and published by ESTATE PUBLICATIONS, Bridewell House, Tenterden, Kent, and based upon the ORDNANCE SURVEY mapping with the permission of The Controller of H. M. Stationery Office.

The publishers acknowledge the co-operation of Hastings Borough Council and Rother District Council in the preparation of these maps.

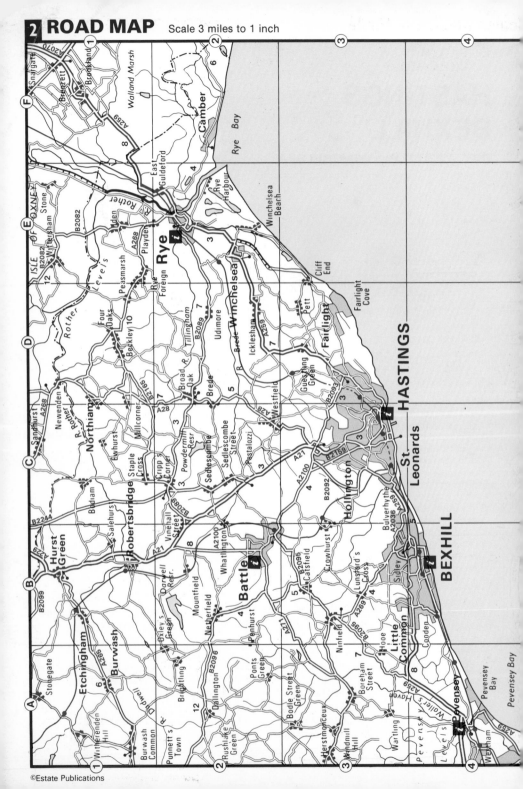

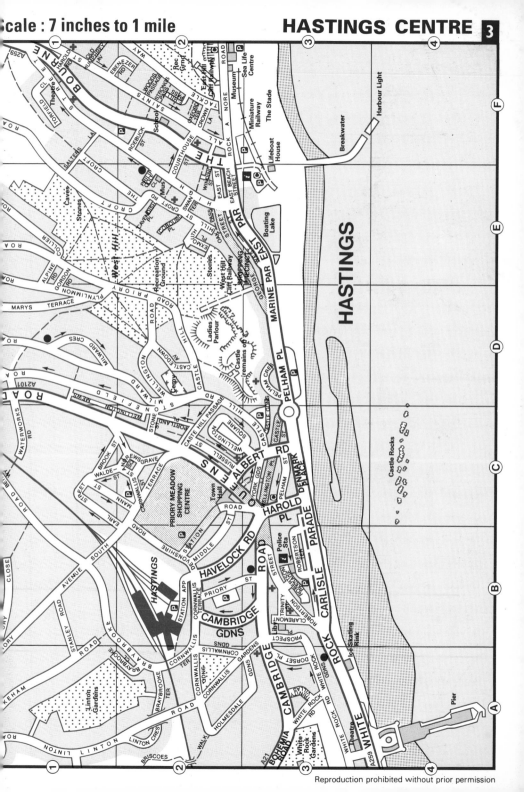

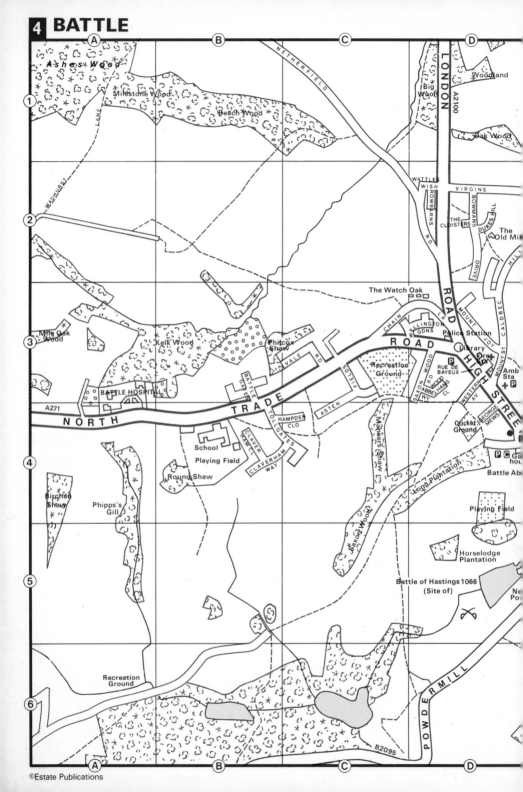

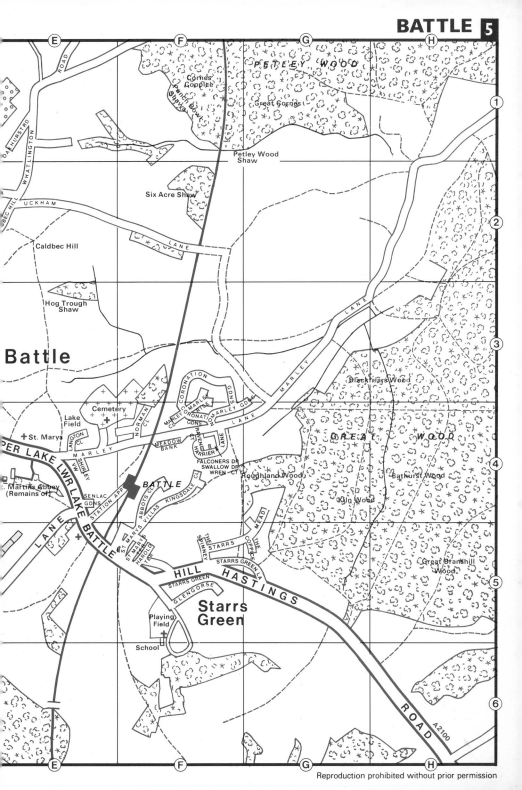

PETLEY WOOD

Cornes Coppice

Great Cornes

E

F

G

H

1

Petley Wood Shaw

ROAD

WHATLINGTON

OAKHURST RD

Six Acre Shaw

UCKHAM

BEC HILL

2

LANE

Caldbec Hill

Hog Trough Shaw

LANE

3

Battle

MARLEY

Blackfriars Wood

CORONATION

Cemetery

Lake Field

St. Marys

NORMAN CL

LANGTON CL

MARLEY

SHIRLEY VW

MARLEY CL

CORONATION GDNS

GDNS

MARLEY GDNS

RAVENSIDE

HARRIER

MEADOW BANK

LANE

LANE

GREAT WOOD

4

Bathurst Wood

FALCONERS DR

SWALLOW DR

WREN CT

Roughland Wood

Kiln Wood

UPPER LAKE

LWR LAKE

Martins Abbey (Remains of)

LANE

BATTLE

SENLAC GDNS

STATION APP

BATTLE

ST MARYS VILLAS

ABBOTS CT

HAROLD TER

KINGSDALE

THE MEAD

THE COPSE

Great Bramshill Wood

5

THE SPINNEY

STARRS

STARRS GREEN LA

STARRS GREEN

GLENGORSE

HILL

HASTINGS

ROAD

Starrs Green

Playing Field

School

A2100

6

E

F

G

H

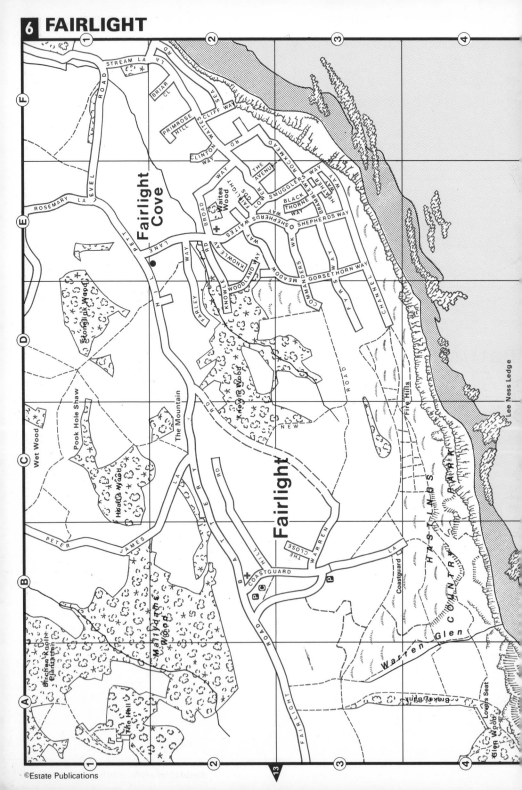

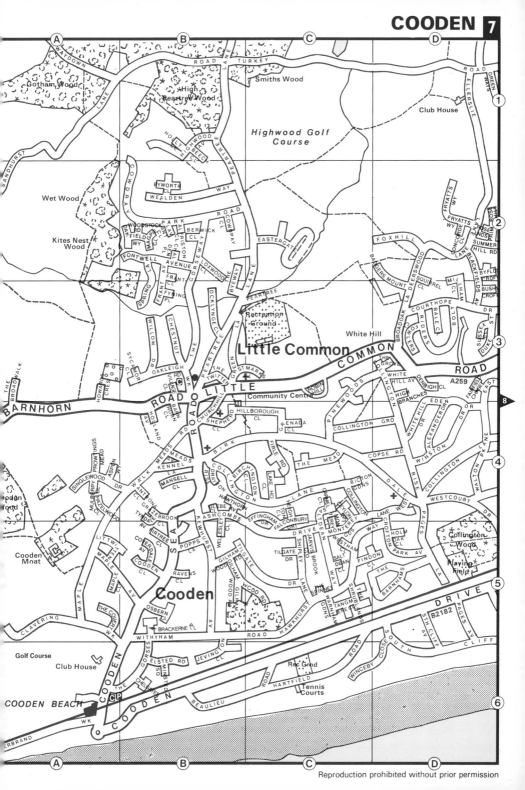

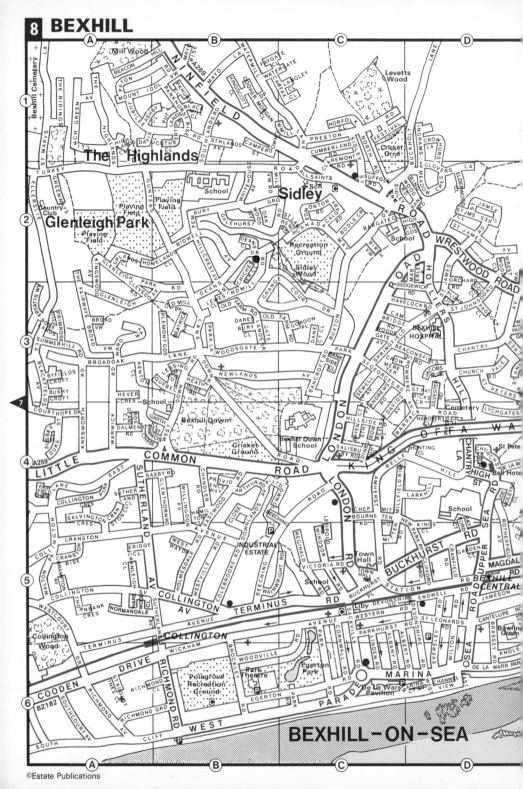

BEXHILL-ON-SEA

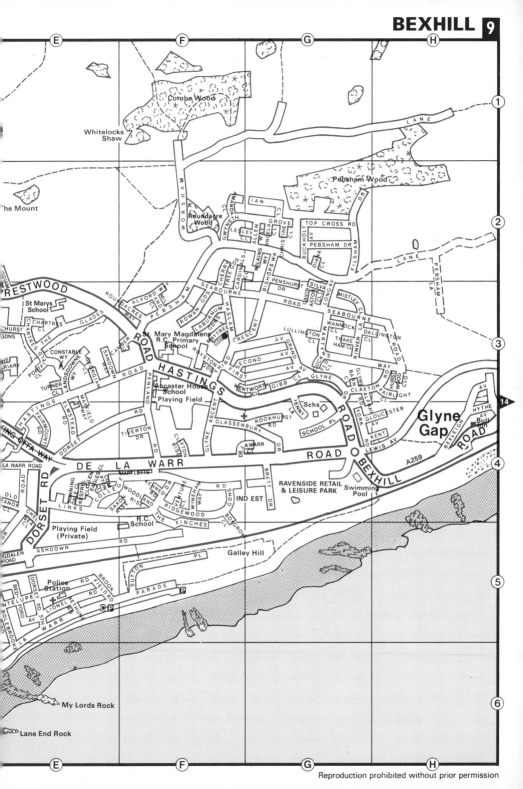

E   F   G   H

1

Combe Wood

Whitelocks
Shaw

LANE

The Mount

Pebsham Wood

2

WORSHAM

Roundacre
Wood

IAN

GWYNETH

LESLEY

ALLEN

ANELA

GROVE

CHRISTINE

TOP CROSS RD

BUCKHOLT

Pebsham Dr

FILSHAM DR

LANE

PEBSHAM
LA

RESTWOOD

St Marys
School

CHARTRES
CL

CHARTRES
GDNS

THE
GLADES

ROUNDACRES
WAY

ALFORD WY

MILL

PEBSHAM

ROAD

CAMBER

SANDOWN

CL
ARGIAN
WAY

LANDSDOWNE

ROAD

SEABOURNE

ROWAN GDNS

LABURNUM

CARDINALS

BISHOPSWK

PENSHURST
DR

ROAD

GAVIN

ASTOR

SILVA

LONG

SEABOURNE

MISTLEY CL

WANNOCK
CL

DALLINGTON
CL

KINVER LA

THAKE
HAM CL

ROAD

3

THE
PRIORY

PORTL
WY

CL

St Mary Magdalens
R.C. Primary
School

CHERR
TREE CLS

MAYTREE

ROYSTON RD
THIRD

CRESCENT

ASLAN

LULLINGTON

GRAND
AV

SECOND
AV

FIRST
AV

GLYNE
CL

SILVA

MARTINS

CL

WAY

DALLINGTON
ROAD

CONSTABLE
WY

TURNER RD

MAYFIELD
WY

ELMSTEAD

DORSET

PENLAND
RD

HASTINGS

ROAD

Ancaster House
School
Playing Field

WENTWORTH
CL

GIBB
CL

GLYNE

ROAD

BAIN
CL

YORK
RD

CLAXTON
CL

GLYNE
ALFRAY

GLOUCESTER

HURST
WOOD

FAIRLIGHT

14

HASTINGS

FAIRMOUNT

GLYNE ASCENT

CLIFTON
RD

TIVERTON
DR

Schs

ROOKHURST RD

GLASSENBURY RD

JENNY

SCHOOL PL

DE LA WARR
CL

DELWARR
DR

Glyne
Gap

BEXLEIGH

HYTHE
AV

Bull
HILL

AV

KENT
RD

LEWIS AV

ROAD

KING OFFA WAY

DE LA WARR

CL

DORSET
RD

LA WARR ROAD

ROAD

LINKS

MARTLETS

SPINNING
DALE

CLOSE

COLLEGE

WOODLAND
RISE

SAXON
RISE

KENNEDY
WAY

VENTURE
WAY

WINEHAM
WAY

RIDGEWOOD

BRETT

THE FINCHES

BOXGROVE

BRETT
RD

GDNS
RD

ROAD

IND EST

RAVENSIDE RETAIL
& LEISURE PARK

Swimming
Pool

A259

ROAD

BEXHILL

4

OLD
MANOR
CL

CHESTER

MGDALEN
ROAD

DORSET RD

ASHDOWN

RD

R.C.
School

Playing Field
(Private)

SUTTON RD

PL

Galley Hill

5

BEDFORD

LUPET

DORSET RD STH

BROOK RD

FIELD RD

LIONEL RD

BETHUNE

Police
Station

P

PARADE

C P

6

My Lords Rock

Lane End Rock

E   F   G   H

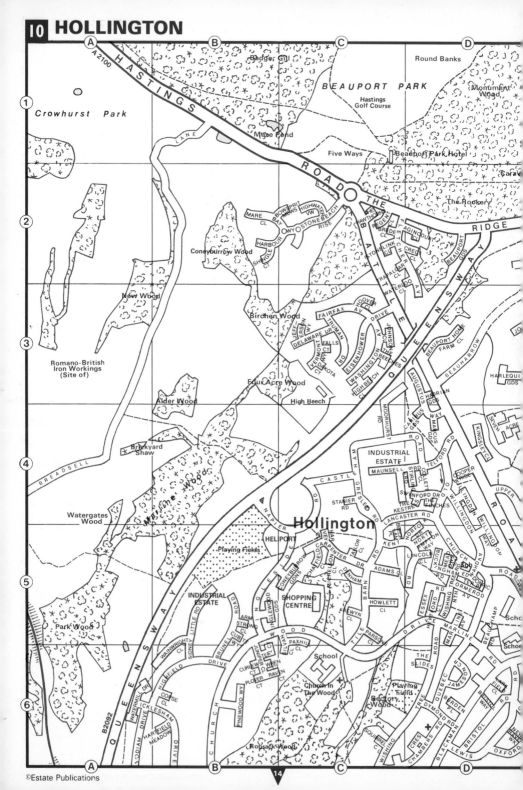

©Estate Publications

14

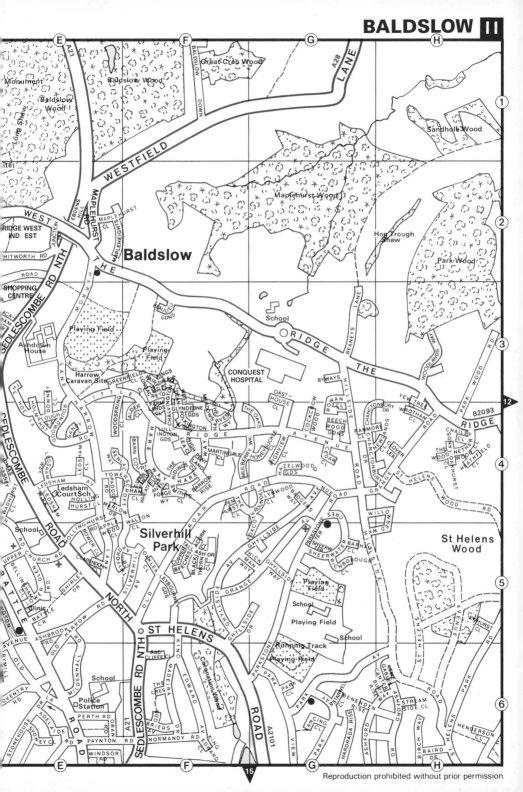

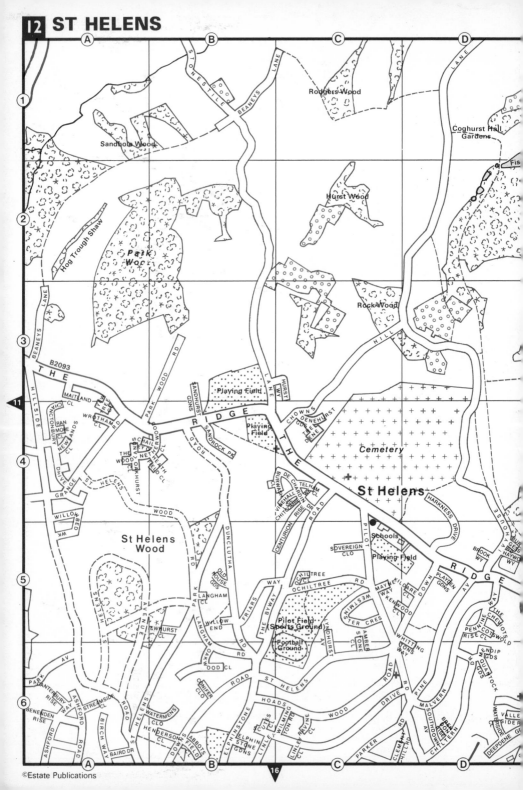

A B C D

1

Rodgers Wood

Coghurst Hall Gardens

Sandhole Wood

Fis

Hurst Wood

2

Hog Trough Shaw

Park Wood

Rock Wood

3

THE

B2093

HILLSIDE

BEANEYS LANE

PARK WOOD RD

RIDGE

SANDHURST GDNS

Playing Field

HURST WY

HILL

CHOWNS GDNS

DENEHURST DENE

11

MAITLAND CL

WROTHAM CL

RANMORE CL

NEWLANDS CL

VICTONBURY CL

CHA

FAIRLIGHT RD

NETHERWOOD

THE WOOD YORK CL

OAKHURST

NETHERFIELD CL

SANDROCK PK

ROAD

Playing Field

THE

DE CHARDIN RISE

TELHAM CL

CHISOMBO RD

St Helens

Cemetery

HARKNESS DRIVE

4

GRANGE ST

ST HELENS

WOOD

WILLOW WK

BED

St Helens Wood

PARK AVENUE

ST HELENS RD

DUNCLUTHA RD

OLD HOUSE GDS

LANGHAM CL

WILLOW END

VINEHALL BURWAY

CENTURION RISE

PILOT

Schools

SOVEREIGN CLO

Playing Field

BROOK WY

BURGESS

HAYWO

RIDGE

THE CHEMISTS

5

ST HELENS AV

NEWHURST CL

LANGHAM RD

OAKWOOD CL

FRIARS RD

THE BWAY

WAY

CALTREE

OCHILTREE

OCHILTREE RD

PILOT

Pilot Field Sports Ground

Football Ground

LINDHURST AV

ISM SIMS

STER CRES

AMBER STONE

MAYFIELD CL

KENWOOD WAY

WHITTINGTONS WAY

PLAYDEN GDNS

CLARE CL

COTSWOLD RISE CL

PENNINE

MENDIP GDS

QUANTOCK GDS

6

PARK AV

CANTERBURY RISE

BENENDEN RISE

ASHFORD WAY

STREAMSIDE CL

BIRCH WAY

BAIRD DR

ASHFORD ROAD

ST HELENS ROAD

HENDERSON CL

WATERMENS CLO

ABBOTS FIELD

JUNIPER CLO

ELPHINSTONE GDNS

ELPHINSTONE RD

LINLEY CL

CUTES

WILMINGTON RD

ALFYNE

ST HELENS RD

HOADS WOOD RD

PARKER RD

CLEMENT HILL RD

PINE

MALVERN AV

M SOUTHDOWN RD

CHILTERN AV

BRECK

CREST

DEEPDENE RD

VALLE

WATERD

SPIDER

16

E F G H

Eight Acre Wood

Hoads Wood

Guestling Green

Five Acre Wood

Brickyard Wood

A259

ROAD

①

oghurst Hall Caravan Site

ond

Bulls Wood

②

OGHURST WOOD

Guestling Hall Youth Hostel

RD

LANE

LANE

ROCK

Ten Acre Wood

White Hart Inn

PETT

RYE

ROAD

③

LANE ROCK

Bachelors Bump

④

JENNERS LA

WINCHELSEA

LA

MARTINEAU

ROAD

LANE

RYE

6

MILL

ROAD

School

AUSTEN

WAY

ROCK

FENDER

CHURCHILL

MONTGOMERY

MOUNTBATTEN

CL

Fairlight Reservoir

④

AV

CL

ROCK

BRICK LANDS

Cemetery

Recreation Grounds

CROWBOROUGH

RD

CROWBOROUGH DR

North Seat

BRO DLANDS

School

Rec Grd

DITCHLING

BRIGHTLING AV

CROWBOROUGH BEACON ROAD

FIRLE

C Picnic

P Site

THE RIDGE

Fire Sta

School

WINCHELSEA RD

GROVE

OLD

RYE

OLD TOP RD

RD

THE

FAIRSTONE CL

MILL LANE

LANE

ROAD

⑤

oghurst rd

VICTORIA

RD

LONDON

RD

School

RICHLAND RD

NEWMANS

THE HEIGHTS

RD

LEEDS

MANHATTEN

FOSTER

MIDDLE

FAIRLIGHT

CLERKMANS

TILEKILN LA

Clinic

FAIRLIGHT

RCY

CLIFTON

GREVILLE

RD

RD

Ore

LONDON

RYE

ROAD

OFFA

FAIRLIGHT

AV

SANDOW

FIELDOWN

SCHOOL RD

GRAYSTON

CHURCH ST

A259

ALFRED

SAXON

CANUTE

EDITH RD

HAMILTON

HAROLD RD

EGOS

RD

BARLEY

⑥

E F G H

17

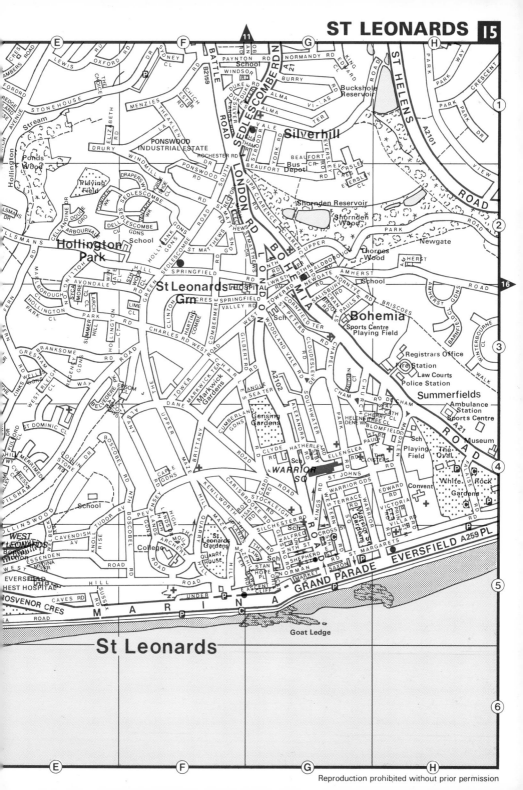

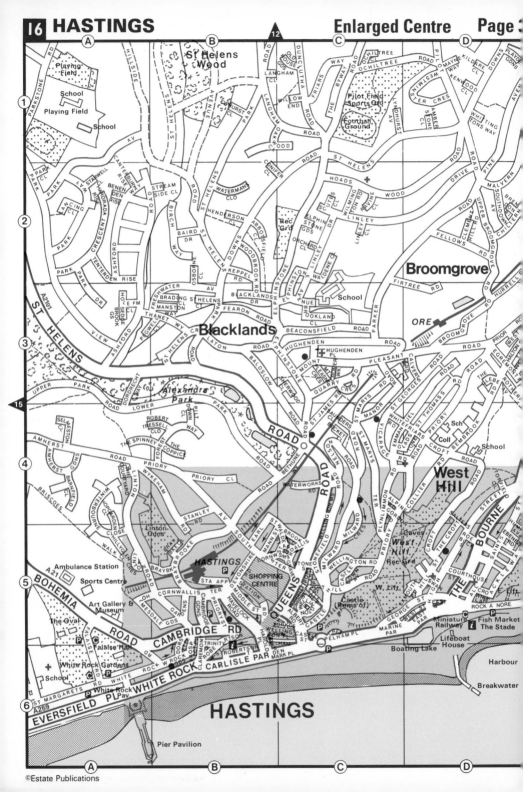

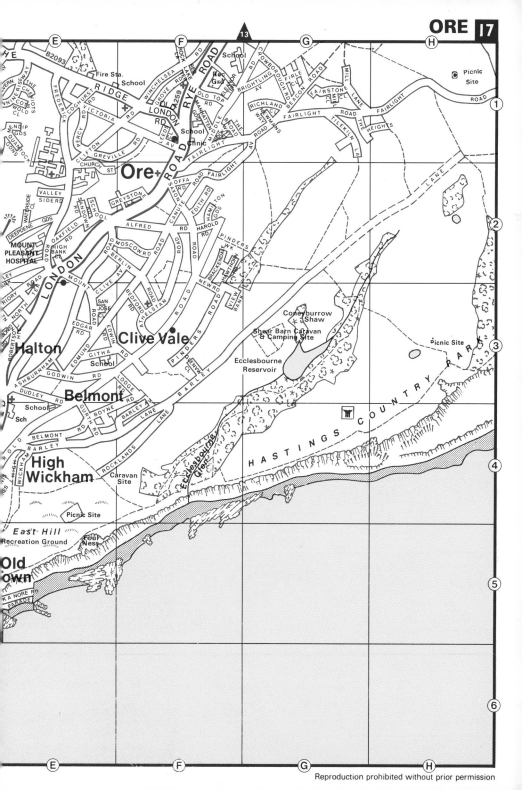

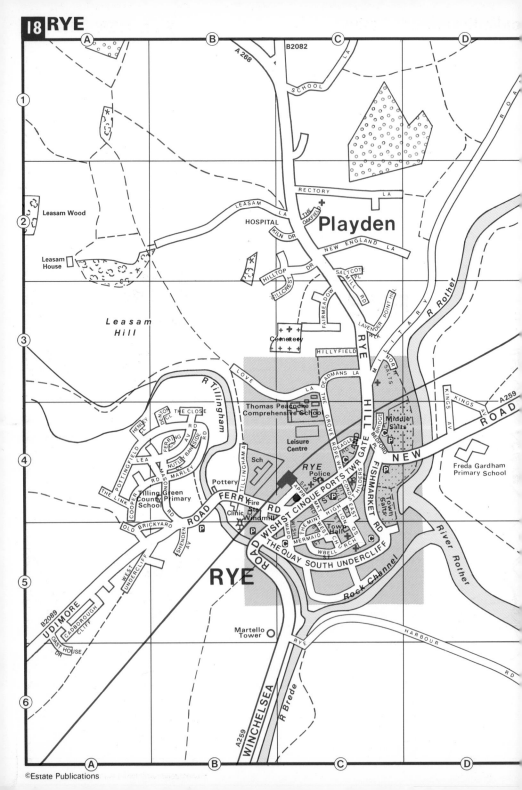

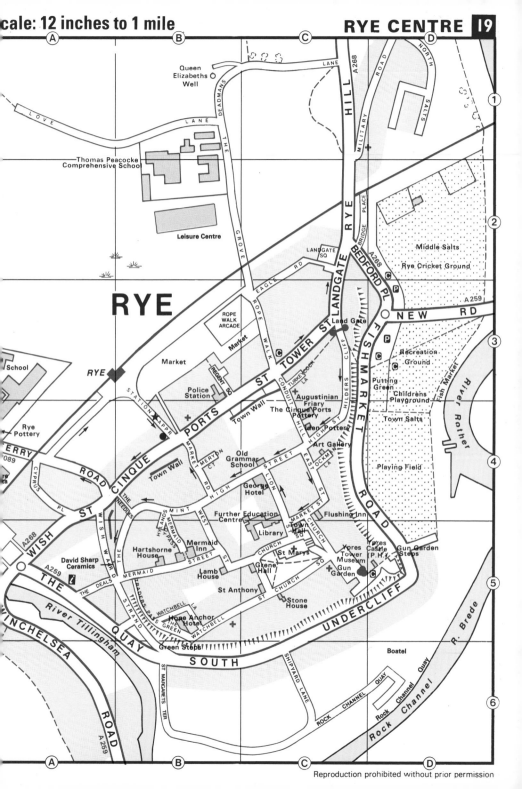

A   B   C   D

1

Queen Elizabeths Well

DEADMANS   LANE

LOVE   LANE

THE   GROVE

HILL   A268

MILITARY   ROAD

NORTH   SALTS

Thomas Peacocke Comprehensive School

Leisure Centre

2

LANDGATE SQ

BRIDGE PLACE

BEDFORD PL

A268

Middle Salts

Rye Cricket Ground

A259

RYE

ROPE WALK ARCADE

Market

EAGLE   RD

ROPE   WALK

Land Gate

LANDGATE

FISHMARKET

NEW   RD

P

Recreation Ground

3

RYE

Market

Police Station

TOWER   ST

PORTS   ST

STATION   APPR

TURKEOCK   LA

Putting Green

Childrens Playground

Rye Pottery

Town Wall

Town Wall

Augustinian Friary

The Cinque Ports Pottery

den Pottery

Art Gallery

CONDUIT   HILL

HTG   LA

HILDERS   CLIFF

EAST   ST

OCKMAN   LA

Town Salts

Playing Field

River Rother

Fish Market

4

School

FERRY   ROAD   089

CINQUE   ST

CYPRUS   PL

ROAD

THE   NEEDLES

MARKET   RD

MERYON   CT

HIGH   STREET

LION   ST

MARKET   ST

Old Grammar School

George Hotel

Further Education Centre

Library

Town Hall

CHURCH   SQ

Flushing Inn

UNDERCLIFF   ROAD

A268

A259

WISH   ST

WISH   WARD

SOMERPASS

MINT

WEST   ST

MERMAID   STREET

THE   DEALS

David Sharp Ceramics

Hartshorne House

Mermaid Inn

Lamb House

St Anthony

St Marys

Grene Hall

CHURCH   LA

CHURCH   SQ

Stone House

Ypres Tower Museum

Gun Garden

Ypres Castle (P.H.)

Gun Garden Steps

5

THE   QUAY

River Tillingham

WINCHELSEA   ROAD

A259

ST   MARGARETS   TER

TRADERS   PASS

STRAND

WATCHBELL   LA

Hope Anchor Hotel

WATCHBELL   ST

Green Steps

SOUTH

SHIPYARD   LANE

Boatel

QUAY

ROCK   CHANNEL   QUAY

Rock Channel

R. Brede

Rock Channel

6

WINCHELSEA

A 259 RD

MILITARY

R Brede

Sewage Works

Land Gate

Caravan Park

R Brede

Castle Farm

TANYARD LANE

FERRY HILL

STATION ROAD

Strand Bridge

ROYAL

MILL

NORTH RD

HIGHAM ST

MILL

CASTLE ST

STRAND ST

BARRACK SQ

Strand Gate

SEA

Waterbridge Place Caravan Park

ROBERTS LANE

GERMAN ST

HIGH STREET

ST THOMASS CH

FERRY LA

Strand Hill

ROAD

OLD RIVER WAY

BACK LA

FRIARS RD

KENT WALK

ST GILES

BACK ROO

HOGTROUGH LA

A 259

SANDROCK HILL

RECTORY LANE

MONKS ROAD

MARKET SQ

The Greyfriars

MILITARY CANAL

MORLAIS PL

GREY FRIARS

HARBOUR FARM

MORLAIS RD

WINCHELSEA

WICKHAM ROCK ROAD

Friars Cliff

ROYAL

SEA RD

WILLOW LANE

Windmill Caravan Park

New Gate

White Lodge Caravan Park

Winchelsea Beach

Winchelsea Sands Carapark

DOGS HILL RD

SMEATONS LANE

THE RIDGE

DONALD WAY

VICTORIA WY

WINDSOR WAY

LEVEL

Rye Bay Caravan Park

C

PETT

Winchelsea Beach Caravan Park

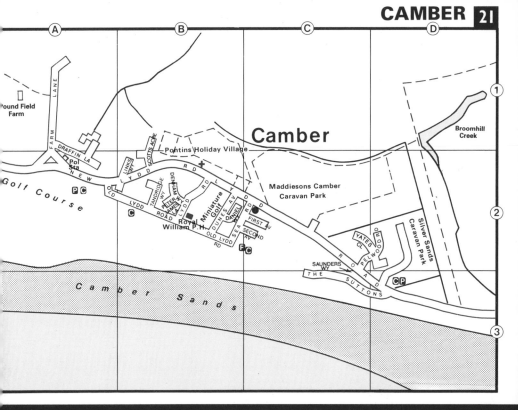

A - Z INDEX TO STREETS
with Postcodes

Crowmere Ter. TN40 8 C3
Cuckfield Clo. TN40 9 G3
Cumberland Rd. TN39 8 C1
Cuthbert Clo. TN39 8 B1
Dalehurst Rd. TN39 8 B2
Dallington Clo. TN40 9 G3
Dalmeny Rd. TN39 8 A4
Dane Court Clo. TN39 8 C3
Daresbury Clo. TN39 8 B3
Davis Clo. TN39 8 A1
De La Warr Ct. TN40 9 F4
De La Warr Par. TN40 8 D6
De La Warr Rd. TN40 8 E4
De Moleyns Clo. TN40 8 D4
Deans Clo. TN39 8 B2
Deans Dri. TN39 8 B3
Deerswood La. TN39 7 D2
Denbigh Clo. TN39 7 D3
Devonshire Rd. TN40 8 D5
Devonshire Sq. TN40 8 C5
Diana Clo. TN40 9 G2
Dorset Rd Sth. TN40 9 E5
Dorset Rd. TN40 9 E5
Down Rd. TN39 8 B3
Downlands Av. TN39 8 B5
Downlands Clo. TN39 8 B5
Drayton Rise. TN39 7 B4
Duke St. TN39 8 A4
Eastergate. TN39 7 C2
Eastwood Rd. TN39 8 B4
Eden Dr. TN39 7 D3
Edinburgh Rd. TN40 8 C4
Edmonton Rd. TN39 8 C2
Effingham Dri. TN39 7 C4
Egerton Rd. TN39 8 B6
Elderwood Clo. TN39 8 D2
Ellerslie La. TN39 8 A2
Elmstead Rd. TN40 9 E4
Elsted Rd. TN39 7 B6
Endwell Rd. TN40 8 D5
Eridge Clo. TN39 8 A5
Eversley Rd. TN40 8 D6
Fairfield Chase. TN39 8 A4
Fairlight Clo. TN40 9 H3
Fairmount Rd. TN40 9 E4
Falconbury Dri. TN39 7 C5
Faygate Clo. TN39 8 B1
Festival Gdns. TN39 8 C1
Filsham Dri. TN40 9 G2
Findon Clo. TN39 7 C5
Fir Tree Clo. TN39 7 B5
Firle Rd. TN39 7 C4
First Av. TN40 9 F3
Fontwell Av. TN39 7 B2
Fowlers Clo. TN39 7 D3
Foxhill. TN39 7 D2
Frant Av. TN39 7 B3
Frant Clo. TN39 7 B2
Fryatts Way. TN39 7 D2
Fyning Pl. TN39 7 B3
*Gainsborough Rd, Lansdowne Way. TN40 9 E3
Galley Hill Vw. TN40 9 F5
Garden Clo. TN40 8 D5
Garth Clo. TN39 8 B4
Gatehouse Clo. TN39 7 B6
Gatelands Dri. TN39 8 B3
Gavin Astor Clo. TN40 9 G3
Georgian Clo. TN40 9 E3
Gibb Clo. TN40 9 G3
Gilham Wood Av. TN39 7 B5
Gilham Wood Rd. TN39 7 B5
Glassenbury Dri. TN40 9 F4
Glebe Clo. TN39 7 B4
Gleneagles Clo. TN40 9 E4
Glenleigh Av. TN39 8 A3
Glenleigh Park Rd. TN39 8 A2
Glenthorn Rd. TN39 8 B4
Gloucester Av. TN40 9 G4
Glovers La. TN39 8 D2
Glyne Ascent. TN40 9 F4
Glyne Barn Clo. TN40 9 G3
Glyne Dri. TN40 9 G3
Goodwood Clo. TN40 8 D3
Gordon Pl. TN39 8 C3
Grand Av. TN40 9 G3
Grange Court Dri. TN39 8 B3
Grazebrook Clo. TN39 7 B4
Green La. TN39 7 B3
Greenways. TN39 8 A2
Grenada Clo. TN39 7 C4
Gunters La. TN39 8 B2
Gwyneth Gro. TN40 9 F2
Hamilton Ter. TN39 8 B4
Hanover Clo. TN40 8 D4
Harewood Clo. TN39 8 A5
Hartfield Rd. TN39 7 C6
Haslam Cres. TN40 9 F3
Hastings Rd. TN40 9 F3
Havelock Rd. TN40 8 C3
Hawkhurst Way. TN39 7 C5
Hawthorn Av. TN39 7 B4
Hazelwood Clo. TN39 7 A4
Heatherdune Rd. TN39 8 B3
Heighton Clo. TN39 7 C4
Herbrand Walk. TN39 7 A6
Hever Cres. TN39 8 A3
High Branches. TN39 7 D3
High Field Gdns. TN39 8 D2
High St. TN40 8 D4
Highlands Clo. TN39 8 A1
Highwood Av. TN39 7 B1
Hillborough Clo. TN39 7 C4
Hillcrest Av. TN39 8 B2
Hillside Rd. TN40 8 C4
Holland Av. TN39 7 B4
Holliers Hill. TN40 8 D2
Holly Clo. TN39 7 B1
Holm Oak Clo. TN39 7 D5
Holmesdale Rd. TN39 8 B5
Homelands Clo. TN39 8 A2
Howards Cres. TN39 7 A3
Hunting Clo. TN40 8 D4
Hurstwood Clo. TN40 9 H3
Ian Clo. TN40 9 G2
Ingrams Av. TN39 8 D1
Jacobs Acre. TN40 8 D3
Jameson Rd. TN40 8 D5
Jarvis Brook Clo. TN39 7 C5
Jevington Clo. TN39 7 B6
Jubilee Rd. TN39 8 A1
Kennedy Rd. TN40 9 F4
Kennel La. TN39 7 B4
Kent Clo. TN40 9 H4
Kenton Clo. TN39 8 A3
Kestrel Clo. TN40 9 E4
Kewhurst Av. TN39 7 B4
King Offa Way. TN40 8 C4
Kings Clo. TN40 8 D5
Kingscott Clo. TN39 8 B1
Kingswood Av. TN39 8 A2
Kinver La. TN40 9 G3
Knebworth Rd. TN39 8 A4
Knole Rd. TN40 8 D6
Laburnum Gdns. TN40 9 F3
Lake House Clo. TN39 7 C4
Langley Clo. TN39 8 C1
Lansdown Way. TN40 9 E3
Larkhill. TN40 8 D4
Lavant Clo. TN39 7 B2
Leasingham Gdns. TN39 8 B3
Leopold Rd. TN39 8 C5
Lesley Clo. TN40 9 F2
Lewes Clo. TN39 8 B3
Lewis Av. TN40 9 G4
Linden Rd. TN40 8 C5
Links Dri. TN40 9 E4
Linley Clo. TN40 8 D5
Lionel Rd. TN40 9 E5
Little Common Rd. TN39 8 A4
Little Twitten. TN39 7 A5
London Rd. TN39 8 C4
Long Av. TN40 9 G3
Loxwood Clo. TN39 7 B2
Lullington Clo. TN40 9 G3
Lychgates Clo. TN40 8 D4
Maberley Rd. TN40 8 D2
Magdalen Rd. TN40 8 D5
Magpie Clo. TN39 7 B2
Manor Rd. TN40 9 E5
Mansell Clo. TN39 7 B4
Maple Av. TN39 7 A5
Maple Clo. TN39 7 A5
Maple Walk. TN39 7 A5
Marina Court Av. TN40 8 D6
Marina. TN40 8 C6
Martyns Way. TN40 9 G3
Mayfield Way. TN40 9 E3
Mayo La. TN39 8 B1
Mayo Rise. TN39 8 B1
Maytree Gdns. TN40 9 F3
Meadow Cres. TN39 8 D2
Meads Av. TN39 7 B4
Meads Rd. TN39 7 B4
Middlesex Rd. TN40 8 D5
Mill View Rd. TN39 8 B2
Milland Clo. TN40 9 F3
Millfield Rise. TN40 8 C4
Millham Clo. TN39 7 D3
Minsted Sq. TN39 7 B6
Mistley Clo. TN40 9 G3
Mitten Rd. TN40 8 C4
Monterey Clo. TN39 7 C4
Monterey Gdns. TN39 7 C5
Morgan Clo. TN39 8 B1
Mount Idol View. TN39 8 A1
Mulberry Clo. TN39 7 A4
New Park Av. TN40 8 D5
Newlands Av. TN39 8 B3
Ninfield Rd. TN39 8 B1
Norfolk Clo. TN39 8 C1
Normandale. TN39 8 A5
North Rd. TN39 8 C1
Oakfield Way. TN39 7 B2
Oakleigh Rd. TN39 7 B3
Oakwood Av. TN39 8 B2
Ocklynge Clo. TN39 7 B3
Old Farm Rd. TN39 8 B3
Old Manor Clo. TN40 9 E4
Orchard Rd. TN40 8 D3
Osbern Clo. TN39 7 B5
Paddock Clo. TN40 8 D3
Pages Av. TN39 7 D5
Pages La. TN39 7 D4
Pankhurst Clo. TN39 8 B1
Pankhurst Rise. TN39 8 B1
Park Av. TN39 8 C6
Park La. TN39 8 B3
Park Rd. TN39 8 C5
Parkhurst Rd. TN40 8 C5
Paton Rd. TN39 8 A1
Peartree La. TN39 7 B1
Pebsham Dri. TN40 9 G2
Pebsham La. TN40 9 F3
Pembury Gro. TN39 8 B2
Penland Rd. TN40 9 F3
Penny La. TN40 9 G3
Penshurst Dri. TN40 9 G2
Piltdown Clo. TN39 8 B4
Pinewoods. TN39 7 C4
Pipers Clo. TN40 8 D4
Plemont Gdns. TN39 8 B3
Plumpton Clo. TN40 8 D3
Popps La. TN39 7 B5
Portfield Clo. TN40 9 E3
Preston Rd. TN39 8 C1
Primrose Hill. TN39 8 A3
Providence Way. TN39 8 B4
Prowtings Mead. TN39 7 A4
Putlands Cres. TN39 8 B1
Quebec Clo. TN39 8 B3
Ravens Clo. TN39 7 B5
Ravenside Retail & Leisure Pk. TN40 9 G4
Rayford Ct. TN40 8 D5
Reginald Rd. TN39 8 C5
Richmond Av. TN39 8 A6
Richmond Clo. TN39 8 A6
Richmond Gro. TN39 8 A6
Richmond Rd. TN39 8 B6
Riders Bolt. TN39 7 D3
Ridgewood Gdns. TN40 9 F4
Ringwood Rd. TN39 8 D2
Robin Hill. TN39 7 C3
Roedean Clo. TN39 8 A4
Rookhurst Rd. TN40 9 G4
Roselands. TN39 8 A3
Rotherfield Av. TN40 8 D5
Roundacres Way. TN40 9 F3
Rowan Gdns. TN40 9 F3
Royston Gdns. TN40 9 F3
Sackville Rd. TN39 8 C5
St Andrews Rd. TN40 8 C4
St Annes Clo. TN40 8 D3
St Augustines Clo. TN39 8 A6
St Davids Av. TN40 8 C4
St Francis Chase. TN39 8 B4
St Georges Rd. TN40 8 C3
St James Av. TN40 8 D2
St James Clo. TN40 8 D2
St James Cres. TN40 8 D2
St James Rd. TN40 8 D3
St Johns Rd. TN40 8 D3
St Lawrence Rd. TN39 8 C2
St Leonards Rd. TN40 8 D5
St Marks Clo. TN39 7 B3
St Marys La. TN39 8 A1
St Patricks Cres. TN40 8 D3
St Peters Cres. TN40 8 D3
Salisbury Rd. TN40 8 C4
Saltdean Clo. TN39 7 C5
Saltdean Way. TN39 7 C4
Salvington Cres. TN39 8 A4
Sandhurst La. TN39 7 A2
Sandown Way. TN40 9 E3
Saxby Rd. TN39 8 B4
Saxon Rise. TN40 9 E4
School Pl. TN40 9 G4
Sea Rd. TN40 8 D6
Seabourne Rd. TN40 9 F3
Second Av. TN40 9 F3
Sedgewick Rd. TN40 8 D3
Sewell Av. TN40 8 C3
Shepherd Clo. TN39 7 B4
Shipley La. TN39 7 C5
Sidley Grn. TN39 8 C2
Sidley St. TN39 8 C1
Silva Clo. TN40 9 G3
Silvester Rd. TN40 8 D4
Singlewood Dri. TN39 7 A4
South Cliff Av. TN39 7 D5
South Cliff. TN39 8 A6
Southcourt Av. TN39 8 A6
Southlands Av. TN39 8 B1
Southlands Rd. TN39 8 B1
Spindlewood Dr. TN39 7 A4
Spring La. TN39 7 B3
Springfield Rd. TN40 8 C3
Squirrel Clo. TN39 7 D2
Station Rd. TN40 8 C5
Suffolk Rd. TN39 8 C2
Summerhill Rd. TN39 8 A3
Sunningdale Clo. TN40 9 E4
Sussex Clo. TN39 8 A4
Sutherland Ave. TN39 8 A4
Sutherland Clo. TN39 8 A4
Sutton Pl. TN40 9 F5
Sycamore Clo. TN39 7 B3
Tangmere Clo. TN39 7 C5
Terminus Av. TN39 8 A6
Terminus Rd. TN39 8 B5
Thakeham Clo. TN40 9 G3
The Barnhams. TN39 7 D5
The Briary. TN40 9 E3
The Broadwalk. TN39 7 A3
The Byeway. TN39 7 B2
The Covert. TN39 7 A5
The Fairways. TN39 8 A2
The Finches. TN40 9 F4
The Glades. TN40 9 E3
The Gorses. TN39 7 A6
The Gorseway. TN39 7 B3
The Grove. TN39 7 D3
The Highlands. TN39 8 A1
The Mead. TN39 7 C4
The Ridings. TN39 8 A1
The Shrublands. TN39 7 C5
The Spinney. TN39 7 C5
The Twitten. TN39 7 B3
Third Av. TN40 9 F3
Thornbank Cres. TN39 8 A5
Tilgate Dri. TN39 7 C5
Tiverton Dri. TN40 9 F4
Top Cross Rd. TN40 9 G2
Town Hall Sq. TN39 8 C5
Turkey Rd. TN39 8 A2
Turner Clo. TN40 9 E3
Tyndale Av. TN39 7 B4
Uplands Clo. . TN39 8 A2
Upper Sea Rd. TN40 8 D5
Venture Clo. TN40 9 F4
Village Clo. TN39 7 B3
Victoria Rd. TN39 8 C5
Wainwright Rd. TN39 8 B5
Walton Pk. TN39 8 A5
Wannock Clo. TN40 9 G3
Ward Way. TN39 8 A3
Warnham Gdns. TN39 7 C5
Warwick Rd. TN39 8 A4
Watergate. TN39 8 B1
Watermill Clo. TN39 8 C1
Watermill La. TN39 8 B1
Wealden Way. TN39 7 B2
Wellesley Clo. TN39 7 B5
Wentworth Clo. TN40 9 F3
West Down Rd. TN39 8 B4
West Parade. TN39 8 B6
Westcourt Dri. TN39 8 A5
Western Rd. TN40 8 C5
Westham Clo. TN39 7 C5
Westville Rd. TN39 8 B5
Westway Dri. TN39 8 B5
White Hill Av. TN39 7 D3
White Hill Dri. TN39 7 D4
Whitehouse Av. TN39 8 B2
Whydown Rd. TN39 7 A1
Wickham Av. TN39 8 B6
Wilkins Way. TN40 9 G2
Willingdon Av. TN39 8 B4
Willow Dri. TN39 7 B3
Wilton Rd. TN40 8 D6
Winceby Clo. TN39 7 D6
Windmill Dri. TN39 8 B3
Windsor Rd. TN39 8 C5
Wineham Way. TN40 9 F4
Winston Dri. TN39 7 D4
Withyham Rd. TN39 7 B5
Woodland Rise. TN40 9 F4
Woodsgate Av. TN40 8 C3
Woodsgate Pk. TN39 8 B3
Woodstock Rd. TN39 7 B2
Woodville Rd. TN39 8 B6
Worsham La. TN40 9 F2
Wrestwood Clo. TN40 8 D2
Wrestwood Rd. TN40 8 D2
Wychurst Gdns. TN40 8 D3
York Rd. TN40 9 G4

CAMBER, RYE WINCHELSEA

Ashenden Av. TN31 18 B5
Back La. TN36 20 B3
Bankside. TN31 18 B4
Barrack Sq. TN36 20 B3
Bedford Pl. TN31 19 C2
Bridge Pl. TN31 19 C2
Cadborough Cliff. TN31 18 A5
Castle St. TN36 20 B3
Church Sq. TN31 19 C5
Cinque Ports St. TN31 19 B4
Conduit Hill. TN31 19 C3
Cooper Rd. TN31 18 A4
Cyprus Pl. TN31 19 A4
Daniel Way. TN31 21 B2
Deadmans La. TN31 19 B1
Denham Way. TN31 21 B2
Denton Clo. TN31 18 B4
Dogs Hill Rd. TN36 20 D5
Donald Way. TN36 20 C5
Draffin La. TN31 21 A1
Dunes Av. TN31 21 B2
Eagle Rd. TN31 19 C3
East St. TN31 19 C4
Fairmeadow. TN31 18 C3
Farm La. TN31 21 A1
Ferring Clo. TN31 18 B4
Ferry Hill. TN36 20 A2
Ferry Rd. TN31 19 A4
First Av. TN31 21 C2
Fishmarket Rd. TN31 19 D3
Frairs Rd. TN36 20 B3
German St. TN36 20 B3
Greyfriars Pl. TN36 20 D3
Harbour Farm. TN36 20 D4
Henley Clo. TN31 18 A4
High St. TN31 19 B4
High St. TN36 20 B3
Higham Grn. TN36 20 B3
Hilders Cliff. TN31 19 C4
Hillcrest. TN31 18 B3
Hillcrest Dri. TN31 18 C3
Hilltop Dri. TN31 18 B2
Hillyfield. TN31 18 C3
Hogtrough La. TN36 20 A3
Hylands Yd. TN31 19 B5
Kent Clo. TN36 20 A3
Kiln Dri. TN31 18 B2
Kings Av. TN31 18 D3
Landgate. TN31 19 C2
Landgate Sq. TN31 19 C2
Lavender Wk. TN31 18 C3
Lea Av. TN31 18 A4
Leasam La. TN31 18 B2
Links Way. TN31 21 B2
Lion St. TN31 19 C4
Love La. TN31 19 A1
Lydd Rd. TN31 21 B2
Market Rd. TN31 19 B4
Market Sq. TN36 20 B3
Market St. TN31 19 C4
Marley Rd. TN31 18 B4
Mason Rd. TN31 18 B4
Mermaid Pass. TN31 19 B5
Mermaid St. TN31 19 B5
Meryon Ct. TN31 19 B4
Military Rd. TN31 19 C1
Mill Rd. TN31 18 C2
Mill Rd. TN36 20 A2
Monks Wk. TN36 20 A4
Morlais Pl. TN36 20 D3
Morlais Ridge. TN36 20 D4
New England La. TN31 18 C2
New Lydd Rd. TN31 21 A2
New Rd. TN31 19.D3
North Salts. TN31 19 D1
North St. TN36 20 B2
Nutley Clo. TN31 18 B4
Oast House Dri. TN31 18 A5
Ockman La. TN31 19 C4
Old Brickyard. TN31 18 A5
Old Lydd Rd. TN31 21 A2
Old River Way. TN36 20 D3
Pelwood Rd. TN31 21 C2
Peter James Clo. TN31 21 B2
Pett Level Rd. TN36 20 C6
Point Hill. TN31 18 C3
Pottingfield Rd. TN31 18 A4
Rectory La. TN31 18 C2
Rectory La. TN36 20 A4
Regent Sq. TN31 19 B3
Roberts Hill. TN36 20 A3
Rock Channel Quay. TN31 19 C6
Rookery La. TN36 20 B3
Rope Wk. TN31 19 C3
Rope Wk Arcade. TN31 19 B3
Royal Military Rd. TN36 20 B2
Rye Harbour Rd. TN31 18 C5
Rye Hill. TN31 19 C1
St Giles Clo. TN36 20 A3
St Margarets Ter. TN31 19 B6
St Thomas St. TN36 20 B3
Saltcote Pl. TN31 18 C2
Sandrock Hill. TN36 20 A3
Saunders Way. TN31 21 C3
School Hill. TN36 20 B2
School La. TN31 18 C1
Scotts Acre. TN31 21 B2
Sea Rd. TN31 21 B2
Sea Rd. TN36 20 D4
Second Av. TN31 21 C2
Shipyard La. TN31 19 C6
Smeatons La. TN36 20 D5
South Undercliff. TN31 19 B6
Station App. TN31 19 B3
Station Rd. TN36 20 A2
Strand. TN31 19 B5
Strand Hill. TN36 20 B3
Tandridge Way. TN31 21 B2
Tanyard La. TN36 20 A2
The Clo. TN31 18 B4
The Deals. TN31 19 A5
The Green. TN31 19 B5
The Grove. TN31 19 B1
The Link. TN31 18 A4
The Mint. TN31 19 B5
The Needles. TN31 19 B4
The Oakfield. TN31 18 C2

The Quay. TN31 19 A5
The Ridge. TN36 20 D5
The Suttons. TN31 21 C3
Tillingham Av. TN31 18 B4
Tower St. TN31 19 C3
Traders Pass. TN31 19 B5
Turkeycock La. TN31 19 C3
Udimore Rd. TN31 18 A5
Victoria Way. TN36 20 C5
Watchbell La. TN31 19 B5
Watchbell St. TN31 19 B5
West St. TN31 19 B4
West Undercliff. TN31 18 A5
Wickham Rock Rd. TN36 20 A5
Willow La. TN36 20 D4
Winchelsea Rd. TN31 19 A5
Windsor Way. TN36 20 C5
Wish St. TN31 19 A5
Wish Ward. TN31 19 A4
Yates Clo. TN31 21 C2

HASTINGS

Abbotsfield Clo. TN34 16 B2
Acorn Clo. TN37 11 F5
Adams Clo. TN38 10 C5
Addington Clo. TN38 14 D4
Adelaide Rd. TN38 11 E6
Agincourt Clo. TN37 10 D2
Albany Rd. TN38 15 F4
Albert Rd. TN34 3 C2
Albourne Clo. TN38 14 D3
Aldborough Rd. TN37 15 G2
Alder Clo. TN37 11 F4
Alexandra Rd. TN37 15 G4
Alfred Rd. TN35 13 E6
Alfred St. TN38 15 G5
All Saints Cres. TN35 17 E4
All Saints St. TN34 3 F2
Alma Ter. TN37 15 G1
Alma Villas. TN37 15 G1
Alpine Rd. TN34 3 E1
Amberstone Clo. TN34 12 C5
Amherst Clo. TN34 15 H2
Amherst Gdns. TN34 15 H3
Amherst Rd. TN34 15 H3
Anglesea Ter. TN38 15 G3
Anvil Ct. TN37 11 F4
Applewood Clo. TN37 11 E5
Arbourvale. TN38 15 E2
Archery Rd. TN38 15 F5
Armstrong Clo. TN38 10 B5
Arnbury Mews. TN38 14 C5
Arnside Rd. TN38 14 C5
Ascot Ms. TN38 15 E4
Ashbrook Rd. TN37 11 E5
Ashburnham Rd. TN35 17 E3
Ashdown Clo. TN38 14 D1
Ashford Rd. TN34 16 A3
Ashford Way. TN34 16 A2
Asten Clo. TN38 14 C4
Athelstan Rd. TN35 17 F3
Augustus Way. TN37 10 D3
Austen Way. TN35 13 F4
Avondale Rd. TN38 15 E2

Badgers Way. TN37 11 G4
Baird Dri. TN34 16 B2
Baldslow Down. TN37 11 F1
Baldslow Rd. TN34 16 B3
Barham Clo. TN37 11 G5
Barley Av. TN35 17 F4
Barley La. TN35 17 E4
Barn Ct. TN37 11 F4
Barnfield Clo. TN34 16 A4
Barrow Rise. TN37 11 F4
Battery Hill. TN35 6 B2
Battle Cres. TN37 11 E5
Battle Rd. TN37 10 C2
Beacon Rd. TN35 13 F5
Beaconsfield Rd. TN34 16 C3
Beanys La. TN34 11 G3
Beauchamp Rd. TN38 10 D5
Beaufort Cres. TN37 15 G1
Beaufort Rd. TN37 15 G2
Beauharrow Rd. TN37 10 D3
Beaulieu Gdns. TN37 11 F3
Beauport Gdns. TN37 10 D2
Beauport Home
Farm Clo. TN37 10 D3
Becket Clo. TN34 16 C4
Beckley Clo. TN38 14 C1
Bedford Rd. TN35 17 F3
Bedgebury Clo. TN38 14 D1
Beecham Pl. TN38 10 C4
Beechwood Gdns. TN37 11 G4
Bellingham Clo. TN37 11 E5
Belmont Rd. TN35 17 E4
Belvedere Pk. TN38 15 E4
Bembrook Rd. TN34 16 D4
Benenden Rise. TN34 11 G6
Berlin Rd. TN35 17 E2
Bethune Way. TN34 16 C4
Bexhill Rd. TN38 14 A6
Birch Way. TN34 16 B2
Blacklands Dri. TN34 16 B3
Blackman Av. TN38 10 D6
Blackthorn Clo. TN37 11 F5
Blackthorne Way. TN35 6 E3
Blomfield Rd. TN37 15 G4
Bluestone Clo. TN38 14 D1
Bodiam Dri. TN38 10 A6
Bohemia Rd. TN34 15 G2
Boscobel Rd. TN38 15 F4
Boscobel Rd Nth. TN38 15 E4
Bourne Pass,
The Bourne. TN34 3 F2
Bower Clo. TN37 11 E5
Bowsprit Ms.. TN38 10 B2
Boyne Rd. TN35 17 E4
Brackendale. TN35 17 F2
Brading Clo. TN34 16 B3
Bramble Way. TN35 6 E3
Branksome Rd. TN38 15 E3
Braybrooke Clo. TN34 3 A2
Braybrooke Rd. TN34 3 A2
Braybrooke Ter. TN34 3 A2
Breadsell La. TN38 10 A4
Brede Clo. TN37 10 C2
Brendon Rise. TN34 12 D6
Briar Clo. TN35 6 F2
Bricklands. TN35 13 E5
Bridge Way. TN38 14 B6
Briers Av. TN34 11 F6
Briers Gdns. TN34 11 F6
Brightling Av. TN35 13 F5
Briscoes Walk. TN34 15 H3
Bristol Rd. TN38 10 D6
Bristol Way. TN38 10 D6
Brittany Rd. TN38 15 F4
Broad Way. TN35 6 E2
Broadlands. TN35 13 E5
Brook St. TN34 3 C1
Brook Way. TN35 12 D5
Brookland Clo. TN34 16 C3
Broomgrove Rd. TN34 16 D3
Brunel Rd. TN38 10 B6
Buckingham Rd. TN38 10 D5
Bulrush Pl. TN38 14 D2
Bulverhythe Rd. TN38 14 B5
Burden Pl. TN38 10 D6
Burgess Rd. TN35 12 D5
Burhill Way. TN38 15 E4
Burry Rd. TN37 15 G1
Burwash Clo. TN34 12 C4
Byways. TN34 11 G3

Calvert Rd. TN34 16 D3
Cambridge Gdns. TN34 3 B2
Cambridge Rd. TN34 3 A3
Canterbury Rise. TN34 11 H6
Canute Rd. TN35 13 E6
Caple Gdns. TN38 15 F4
Cardiff Rd. TN38 15 G4
Carinus Gdns. TN37 10 D4
Carisbrooke Rd. TN38 15 F4
Carlisle Par. TN34 3 B3
Carpenter Dri. TN38 10 C5
Castle Hill Passage. TN34 3 C2
Castle Hill Rd. TN34 3 C3
Castle Gdns. TN34 3 C3
Castle St. TN34 3 C3
Castledown Av. TN34 3 D2
Castleham Rd. TN38 10 C4
Catsfield Clo. TN38 14 C1
Cavendish Av. TN38 15 E5
Cavendish Pl. TN34 3 E2
Caves Rd. TN38 15 E5
Cedar Clo. TN37 11 G4
Cellandine Dri. TN38 15 E2
Centurion Rise. TN34 12 C5
Chailey Clo. TN34 12 A4
Chalvington Dri. TN37 11 F4
Chambers Cres. TN38 10 D6
Chambers Rd. TN38 10 D6
Chanctonbury Dri. TN34 11 G4
Channel Way. TN35 6 D3
Chapel Park Rd. TN37 15 G3
Charles Rd. TN38 15 F3
Charles Rd West. TN38 15 F3
Chatfield Clo. TN38 10 C5
Chatham Rd. TN37 15 G1
Cherry Tree Clo. TN37 15 G4
Chichester Rd. TN38 15 F1
Chiltern Dri. TN34 12 D6
Chitcombe Walk. TN34 12 C4
Chowns Hill. TN35 12 C4
Church Rd. TN37 15 G3
Church St. TN35 13 E6
Church Wood Dri. TN38 10 B6
Churchill Av. TN35 13 E5
Churchwood Way. TN38 14 D1
Claremont. TN34 3 B3
Clarence Rd. TN37 15 G2
Clarendon Clo. TN37 11 E5
Clement Hill Rd. TN34 16 D2
Cliff Way. TN35 6 F2
Clifton Road. TN35 13 E6
Cliftonville Rd. TN38 14 B6
Cliftonville Way. TN38 14 C5
Clinton Cres. TN38 15 F3
Clinton Way. TN35 6 F2
Clive Av. TN35 17 E3
Cloudesley Rd. TN37 15 G3
Cloverlea. TN34 11 H4
Clyde Rd. TN38 15 G4
Coastguard La. TN35 6 B2
Cobourg Pl. TN34 3 E2
Cockcrow Wood. TN37 11 G4
Coghurst Rd. TN35 13 E5
Collett Clo. TN38 10 D4
Collier Rd. TN34 3 E1
Collinstone Rd. TN38 15 E4
Collinswood Dri. TN38 14 D5
Combermere Rd. TN38 15 F3
Commanders Wk. TN35 6 D3
Coneyburrow Gdns. TN38 10 C5
Conifer Clo. TN34 12 B6
Conqueror Rd. TN38 14 C5
Cooper Rise. TN37 10 D4
Copper Beeches. TN37 11 F5
Copse Clo. TN38 10 B6
Cornfield Ter. TN37 15 G3
Cornwallis Gdns. TN34 3 A2
Cornwallis St. TN34 3 C2
Cornwallis Ter. TN34 3 A2
Cotswold Clo. TN34 12 D5
Courthouse St. TN34 3 E2
Coventry Rd. TN38 11 E6
Cowden Walk. TN38 15 E2
Cranbrook Rd. TN37 15 G3
Crecy Clo. TN37 10 D2
Croft Rd. TN34 3 E2
Cromer Walk. TN34 16 C3
Cross St. TN37 15 G5
Crowborough Rd. TN35 13 F5
Crowhurst Rd. TN38 14 A1
Crown La. TN34 3 F2
Cubitt Way. TN38 10 B5
Cumberland Gdns. TN38 15 F4
Curlew Ct. TN38 10 B6
Cypress Clo. TN38 15 E4

Dakota Ct. TN38 10 C3
Dane Rd. TN38 15 F3
Darwell Clo. TN38 14 C2
De Cham Av. TN37 15 H3
De Cham Rd. TN37 15 G3
De Chardin Rd. TN34 12 C4
Deepdene Gdns. TN35 17 E2
Delaware Dri. TN37 10 C3
Dell Clo. TN38 15 E2
Denehurst Gdns. TN35 12 C4
Denham Clo. TN38 10 C5
Denmark Pl. TN34 3 C3
Devonshire Rd. TN34 3 B2
Ditchling Dri. TN35 13 B5
Dittons Mews. TN38 14 C1
Donric Pl. TN38 10 D5
Dordrecht Way. TN34 16 A3
Dorset Pl. TN34 3 A3
Douce Gro. TN38 15 E2
Downey Clo. TN37 11 E4
Downs Rd. TN34 16 B2
Drapers Way. TN38 15 F2
Drury La. TN38 15 E1
Dudley Rd. TN35 17 E3
Duke Rd. TN37 15 F1
*Duke Ms, Duke St. TN37 15 F1
Duke St. TN37 15 F1
Duke Ter. TN37 15 F1
Dunclutha Rd. TN34 12 B5
Dymond Rd. TN38 10 D6

Earl St. TN34 3 C1
East Ascent. TN38 15 G5
East Beach St. TN34 3 E2
*East Bourne St,
The Bourne. TN34 3 F2
East Hill Pass. TN34 3 F2
East Par. TN34 3 E3
East St,
St Leonards. TN37 15 G5
East St, Hastings. TN34 3 E2
Ebdens Hill. TN37 11 E2
Ebenezer Rd. TN34 3 F1
Edgar Rd. TN35 17 E3
Edinburgh Rd. TN38 14 C4
Edith Rd. TN35 13 F6
Edmund Rd. TN35 17 E3
Edward Rd. TN37 15 H4
Edward Ter. TN38 10 D5
Edwin Rd. TN35 17 E3
Egremont Pl. TN34 16 D3
Eisenhower Dri. TN37 10 C3
Eleanor Ter. TN35 17 F1
Elizabeth Rd. TN38 15 E1
Ellenslea Rd. TN37 15 G4
Elphinestone Gdns. TN34 12 B6
Elphinestone Rd. TN34 12 B6
Elphinstone Av. TN34 16 C3
Epsom Clo. TN38 15 F3
Emmanuel Rd. TN34 16 C4
Essenden Rd. TN38 15 E5
Essex Rd. TN38 10 D5
Eversfield Pl. TN37 15 H5
Eversley Clo. TN37 15 G2
Eversley Cres. TN37 15 G2
Eversley Rd. TN37 15 G1
Ewhurst Clo. TN34 16 B1
Exmouth Pl. TN34 3 E2

Fairfax Av. TN37 10 C3
Fairfield Rd. TN37 11 F3
Fairlight Av. TN35 13 F6
Fairlight Gdns. TN35 6 E2
Fairlight Rd. TN35 13 F6
Fairstone Clo. TN35 13 G5
Falaise Rd. TN34 16 A5
Falls Ct. TN38 10 C3
Farley Bank. TN35 17 E2
Farley Way. TN35 6 D2
Farmlands Clo. TN37 11 F4
Fearon Rd. TN34 16 B3
Fellows Rd. TN34 16 D2
Fen Court. TN38 14 D3
Fern Rd. TN38 15 E3
Fernside Av. TN38 14 D3
Fieldway. TN38 14 C3
Filsham Rd. TN38 14 D5
Filsham Valley. TN38 15 E4
Firle Clo. TN35 13 F5
Firtree Rd. TN34 16 C2
Fletcher Av. TN37 10 C2
Flimwell Clo. TN38 14 C1
Folkington Gdns. TN37 11 F4
Ford Rd. TN38 15 E1
Forest Way. TN34 16 B4
Forge Way. TN37 11 F4
Foxcote. TN37 11 G5
Frederick Rd. TN35 13 E5
Freshfields. TN38 14 A5
Freshwater Av. TN34 16 B3
Frewyn Clo. TN38 10 C5
Friars Way. TN34 12 B5
Fulford Clo. TN38 15 E4
Fyrsway. TN35 6 D3

Ganton Pl. TN38 14 D4
Gensing Rd. TN38 15 G5
George St. TN34 3 D3
*Georgian Walk,
Fernside Av. TN38 14 D3
Ghyllside Av. TN34 11 F5
Ghyllside Dri. TN34 11 F5
Ghyllside Way. TN34 11 G5
Gilbert Rd. TN38 15 F3
Gillsmans Dri. TN38 14 D2
Gillsmans Hill. TN38 14 D2
Gillsmans Park. TN38 14 D3
Githa Rd. TN35 17 E3
Gladstone Ter. TN34 16 C4
Gleneagles Dri. TN38 14 D4
Glenview Clo. TN35 17 F3
Glyndebourne
Gdns. TN37 11 F4
Godwin Rd. TN35 17 E3
Gordon Rd. TN34 3 D1
Gorsethorn Way. TN35 6 E3
Grand Parade. TN38 15 G5
Grange Av. TN34 11 F5
Grange Rd. TN34 11 G4
Graystone La. TN35 13 E6
Greenfields Clo. TN37 11 E3
Gresham Way. TN38 15 E3
Gresley Rd. TN38 10 C4
Greville Rd. TN35 13 E6
Grosvenor Cres. TN38 14 D5
Grosvenor Gdns. TN38 14 D5
Grove Rd. TN35 13 E5
Gurth Rd. TN35 17 E4

Hadrian Gdns. TN37 10 D3
Halton Cres. TN34 16 D3
Halton Pl. TN34 17 E3
Halton Ter. TN34 16 D3
Hamilton Gdns. TN35 13 F6
Harbour Way. TN38 10 B2
Hardrada Rise. TN34 16 A2
Hardwicke Rd. TN34 16 D3
Hare Way. TN37 11 F4
Harkness Dri. TN35 12 D4
Harlequin Gdns. TN37 10 D3
Harley Shute Rd. TN38 14 C5
Harley Way. TN38 14 C5
Harold Pl. TN34 3 C3
Harold Rd. TN35 17 E4
Harrow La. TN37 11 E2
Hartfield Meadow. TN38 10 A6
Harting Combe. TN38 15 F3
Harvest Way. TN37 11 F4
Harvey Clo. TN38 10 C5
Hastings Rd. TN38 10 A1
Havelock Rd. TN34 3 B2
Haven Rd. TN38 14 B5
Hawthorn Rd. TN35 17 F2
Haywood Way. TN35 12 D5
Hazelwood Gdns. TN37 11 G4
Heather Way. TN35 6 E3
Heathfield Clo. TN34 12 B4
Helensdene Walk. TN37 15 G4
Henderson Clo. TN34 16 B2
Heron Clo. TN38 14 C3
Hertford Clo. TN38 10 D5
*Hestingas Plat,
Ebenezer Rd. TN34 16 D5
Hickman Way. TN34 11 G5
High Bank Clo. TN35 17 E2
High Beech Clo. TN37 10 C3
High St. TN34 3 E2
High Wickham. TN35 17 E4
Highfield Dri. TN38 10 B6
Highlands Dri. TN38 15 F4
Highlands Gdns. TN38 15 F4
Highlea Clo. TN37 11 F4
Highview Clo. TN37 11 G4
Highwater Vw. TN38 10 C2
Hill Rd. TN35 6 B2
Hill St. TN34 3 E2
Hillside Rd. TN34 11 G3
Hillyglen Clo. TN34 16 A5
Hoads Wood Rd. TN34 12 B6
Hole Farm Clo. TN34 16 A3
Hollinghurst Clo. TN37 11 E4
Hollinghurst Rd. TN37 11 E5
Hollington Court. TN38 15 E3
Hollington Old La. TN38 10 D5
Hollington Park Clo. TN38 15 E3
Hollington Park Rd. TN38 15 E2
Hollybank Gdns. TN38 15 F2
Holmesdale Gdns. TN34 3 A2
Holmhurst La. TN37 11 E4
Honeysuckle Clo. TN37 11 G4
Hoover Clo. TN37 10 C3
Hopgarden Clo. TN34 16 A4
Horntye Rd. TN37 15 G2
Horseshoe Clo. TN38 15 F2
Howlett Clo. TN38 10 C5
Hughenden Pl. TN34 16 C3
Hughenden Rd. TN34 16 C3
Hurrell Rd. TN34 16 D3
Hurst Way. TN35 12 C3

Icklesham Dri. TN38 10 A6
INDUSTRIAL ESTATES:
Ponswood
Ind Est. TN38 15 F1
Ridge West
Ind Est. TN37 11 E2
Ingleside. TN38 10 B5
Inglewood Gdns. TN38 10 B5
Ironlatch Clo. TN38 14 D2
Ivyhouse La. TN35 12 D5

Jameson Cres. TN38 10 D6
Jefferson Way. TN37 10 C3
Jenners La. TN35 13 F3
John Macadam
Way. TN37 10 D3
Johnson Clo. TN37 10 C3
Junction Rd. TN37 11 E2
Juniper Clo. TN38 10 B6

Keats Clo. TN38 14 D5
Kenilworth Rd. TN38 15 F4
Kent Rd. TN38 10 C5
Kenwood Clo. TN34 12 C5
Keppel Rd. TN34 16 B2
Keymer Clo. TN38 14 D5
Kildare Clo. TN34 12 D5
King Edward Av. TN34 11 F6
King Edward Clo. TN34 11 F6
Kings Rd. TN37 15 G4
Kingsdale Clo. TN37 11 F3
Kingsley Clo. TN37 10 D4
Kite Clo. TN38 14 D3
Knoll Rise. TN38 15 E5
Knowle Av. TN35 6 E2
Knowle Rd. TN35 6 D2

Laleham Clo. TN37 11 F4
Lancaster Rd. TN38 10 C4
Lancing Clo. TN34 11 G6
Langham Clo. TN34 12 B5
Langham Rd. TN34 12 B5
Larch Clo. TN38 15 E3
Larkfield Clo. TN38 10 D6
Laton Rd. TN34 16 B3
Ledsham Av. TN37 11 E4
Ledsham Clo. TN37 11 E4
Ledsham Pk. TN37 11 E4
Ledsham Way. TN37 11 E4
Leeds Clo. TN35 13 E6
Lewis Rd. TN38 10 D6
Leybourne Gdns. TN37 11 F5
Lime Clo. TN38 15 F3
Lincoln Clo. TN38 10 D5
Linley Clo. TN34 16 C2
Linley Dri. TN34 16 C2
Linton Cres. TN34 3 A2
Linton Rd. TN34 3 A1
Little Ridge Av. TN37 11 E3
Lodge Rd. TN35 17 F3
London Rd. TN37 15 F2
Longacre Clo. TN37 11 F3
Lovat Mead. TN38 14 C5
Lower Glen Rd. TN37 11 E5
Lower Park Rd. TN34 16 A4

Lower South Rd. TN37 15 G2
Lower Waites La. TN35 6 E2
Lullington Gdns. TN37 11 F4
Lyndhurst Av. TN34 12 C5
Lynwood Clo. TN37 11 G4
Lytham Clo. TN38 14 D3

Madeira Dri. TN34 11 F6
Magdalen Rd. TN37 15 H4
Magpie Clo. TN38 14 C3
Maitland Clo. TN34 12 A3
Malvern Way. TN34 12 D6
Manhatten Gdns. TN35 17 F1
Mann St. TN34 3 C2
Manor Rd. TN34 16 C4
Manston Way. TN34 16 A2
Maple Heights. TN37 11 E2
Maplehurst Clo. TN37 11 E2
Maplehurst Rd. TN37 11 E2
Marcus Gdns. TN37 10 D4
Mare Bay Clo. TN38 10 B2
Marina. TN38 15 E5
Market St. TN38 15 G5
Markwick Ter. TN38 15 F3
Marlborough Clo. TN38 15 E2
Marline Av. TN38 10 D5
Marline Rd. TN38 10 D5
Marlow Dri. TN37 11 E4
Martineau La. TN35 13 G4
Martingale Clo. TN37 11 F4
Maudlin Ct. TN37 15 G3
Maunsell Rd. TN38 10 C4
Mayfield La. TN34 14 B1
Mayne Way. TN34 12 C5
Maze Hill. TN38 15 F4
Mazehill Ter. TN38 15 F5
Meadow Way. TN35 6 E3
Meadows Clo. TN38 10 D5
Medina Ter. TN38 15 E4
Mendip Gdns. TN38 12 D6
Menzies Rd. TN38 15 F1
Mercatoria. TN38 15 G5
Merrimede Clo. TN38 15 G5
Mews Rd. TN34 15 G5
Michele Clo. TN38 15 F2
Michelson Clo. TN38 10 C5
Middle Rd. TN35 13 F6
Middle St. TN38 16 B5
Mildenhall Dri. TN37 11 E6
Mill Clo. TN35 13 G5
Mill La. TN35 13 G5
Milward Cres. TN34 3 D2
Milward Rd. TN34 3 D2
Montgomery Rd. TN35 13 F4
Moorhurst Rd. TN38 10 C4
Moscow Rd. TN35 17 F2
Mount Pleasant
    Cres. TN34 16 C3
Mount Pleasant
    Rd. TN34 16 C3
Mount Rd. TN35 17 E2
Mountbatten Clo. TN35 13 F4
Muirfield Rise. TN38 14 D4
Mulberry Wk. TN37 11 H5

Napier Rd. TN38 10 B4
Nelson Rd. TN34 16 C4
Netherwood Clo. TN34 12 A4
New Rd, Fairlight. TN35 6 C3
New Rd, Ore. TN35 17 F2
Newgate Rd. TN37 15 G2
Newhaven Walk. TN38 10 D4
Newlands Clo. TN34 11 H4
Newmans Way. TN35 13 F4
Nook Clo. TN35 17 F1
Norfolk Dri. TN38 10 D5
Norman Rd. TN37 15 G5
Normandy Rd. TN34 11 F6
North Rd. TN37 15 G2
North St. TN38 15 G5
North Ter. TN34 17 E3
Northampton Way. TN38 10 D5
Northiam Rise. TN34 14 C1

Oak Pass. TN34 3 E2
Oakfield Rd. TN34 13 E6
Oakhurst Clo. TN34 12 A4
Oaklea Clo. TN37 11 F5
Oakwood Clo. TN37 12 B6
Oasthouse Clo. TN37 11 G3
Oban Rd. TN37 11 E6
Ochiltree Clo. TN34 12 C5
Ochiltree Rd. TN34 12 C5
Offa Rd. TN35 13 F5
Old Church Rd. TN38 10 D4
Old Harrow Rd. TN37 11 H3
Old House Gdns. TN34 12 B5

Old Humphrey Av. TN34 3 F1
Old London Rd. TN35 17 E4
Old Roar Rd. TN37 11 F5
Old Top Rd. TN35 13 F5
Orchard Clo. TN34 16 C2
Ormerod Av. TN34 10 D5
Osborne Clo. TN34 16 B2
Oxford Clo. TN38 10 D6
Oxford Ter. TN34 3 F2

Paddock Rd. TN37 11 E4
Park Av. TN34 11 G6
Park Clo. TN34 11 G6
Park Cres. TN34 11 G6
Park Dri. TN34 16 A2
Park View. TN34 11 G6
Park Way. TN34 11 G6
Park Wood Rd 12 A4
Parker Rd. TN34 16 C3
Parkstone Rd. TN34 11 G5
Parkstone Ter. TN34 11 G5
Parsons Clo. TN38 10 C5
Paxhill Clo. TN38 10 C5
Paynton Rd. TN37 11 F6
Pegwell Clo. TN34 16 A3
Pelham Cres. TN34 3 D3
Pelham Pl. TN34 3 D3
Pelham St. TN34 3 C3
Penhurst Clo. TN37 11 F4
Pennine Rise. TN34 12 D5
Pentland Clo. TN37 11 F4
Percy Rd. TN35 13 E6
Perth Rd. TN34 11 E6
Peter James La. TN38 6 B1
Pett Level Rd. TN35 6 E1
Pett Rd. TN35 13 H2
Pevensey Rd. TN38 15 F4
Philip Cole Clo. TN38 3 E2
Pilot Rd. TN34 12 C5
Piltdown Clo. TN34 16 B4
Pinders Clo. TN35 17 F3
Pinders Walk. TN35 17 F2
Pine Av. TN34 12 D6
Pinewood Way. TN38 10 B6
Playden Gdns. TN34 3 E1
Plough La. TN37 11 E4
Plover Clo. TN38 10 B6
Plynlimmon Rd. TN34 3 D1
Ponswood
    Ind Est. TN38 15 F1
Ponswood Rd. TN38 15 F2
Portland Pl. TN34 3 C2
Portland Steps. TN34 16 C5
Primrose Hill. TN35 6 E2
Princes Rd. TN37 15 H4
Priory Av. TN34 3 A1
Priory Clo. TN34 3 B1
Priory Meadow
    Shopping Centre. TN34 3 C2
Priory Rd. TN34 3 D2
Priory St. TN34 3 B2
Prospect Pl. TN34 3 B3

Quantock Gdns. TN34 12 D6
Quarry Cres. TN34 16 C3
Quarry Hill. TN38 15 F4
Quarry House. TN38 15 F5
Quarry Rd. TN34 16 C3
Quebec Rd. TN38 10 D6
*Queens Par,
    York Gdns. TN34 3 C3
Queens Rd. TN34 3 C3
Queensway. TN38 10 A6

Radcliffe Clo. TN37 11 F6
Radnor Mews. TN34 14 D1
Ranmore Clo. TN34 11 G4
Raven Ct. TN34 10 B6
Ravine Clo. TN34 3 E1
Rectory Clo. TN38 15 F2
Redgeland Rise. TN38 14 D1
Redlake Ter. TN35 17 F1
Reedswood Rd. TN38 14 C3
Regency Gdns. TN38 15 E3
Regent Clo. TN37 10 C2
Richborough Clo. TN34 11 G5
Richland Clo. TN35 13 F5
Ridge West
    Ind wood Rise. TN37 11 E2
Ridgewood Mews. TN38 14 D1
Robert Tressell Clo. TN38 16 B4
Robertson Pass. TN34 3 B3
Robertson St. TN34 3 B3
Robertson Ter. TN34 3 B3
Robertsons Hill. TN34 3 C2
Robsack Av. TN38 14 C1
Rochester Rd. TN37 15 F1
Rock A Nore Rd. TN34 3 F3

Rock Clo. TN35 13 E5
Rock La. TN35 13 E1
Rocklands La. TN35 17 E4
Rockmead Rd. TN34 6 E3
Roebuck St. TN34 3 F3
Rosemary La. TN35 6 E1
Rotherfield Av. TN34 16 D3
Rothsay Rd. TN34 15 F4
Roundwood Rd. TN37 11 E4
Rowan Clo. TN37 11 G4
Rushmere Rise. TN34 16 C2
Russell St. TN34 3 C2
Rye Rd. TN35 13 F5
Rymill Rd. TN38 11 E6

St Andrews Sq. TN34 3 C2
St Catherines Clo. TN37 15 H4
St Dominic Clo. TN34 15 E4
St Georges Rd. TN34 16 C4
St Helens Av. TN34 12 A5
St Helens Court. TN34 16 B3
St Helens Cres. TN34 16 B3
St Helens Down. TN34 12 B6
St Helens Park Rd. TN34 12 A6
St Helens Rd. TN34 11 F5
St Helens Wood Rd. TN34 12 A4
St James Rd. TN34 16 C4
St Johns Rd. TN37 15 G4
St Margarets Rd. TN37 15 G5
St Margarets Ter. TN34 15 H5
St Marys Rd. TN34 3 D1
St Marys Ter. TN34 3 D1
St Matthews Dri. TN38 15 G2
St Matthews Gdns. TN38 15 F2
St Matthews Rd. TN34 15 F2
St Pauls Pl. TN37 15 G3
St Pauls Rd. TN37 15 G3
St Peters Rd. TN37 15 G3
St Saviours Rd. TN38 14 D5
St Thomas's Rd. TN34 16 D4
St Vincents Rd. TN37 14 D5
Salcey Clo. TN38 14 D1
Salehurst Gdns. TN38 14 C1
Salisbury Rd. TN34 15 G3
Salters La. TN34 3 E1
San Jose Clo. TN35 17 E3
Sandhurst Gdns. TN34 12 B3
Sandown Rd. TN35 13 E6
Sandrock Pk. TN34 16 B4
Sandwich Dri. TN38 14 D4
Sandy Clo. TN37 11 E4
Saunders Clo. TN34 16 C4
Saxon Road. TN35 13 E6
Saxon St. TN37 15 G5
School Rd. TN35 13 E6
Scutes Clo. TN34 16 C2
Sea Rd,
    Fairlight Cove. TN35 6 F2
Sea Rd,
    St Leonards. TN38 15 E5
Seaside Rd. TN38 14 D5
Sedgebrook Gdns. TN34 16 A3
Sedlescombe Gdns. TN38 15 F2
Sedlescombe
    Rd Nth. TN37 11 E3
Sedlescombe
    Rd Sth. TN38 15 F2
Selmeston Clo. TN34 16 A4
Senlac Way. TN34 11 E4
Seven Acre Clo. TN37 10 D4
Sheerwater Cres. TN34 11 G5
Sheerwater Ter. TN34 11 G5
Shepherd St. TN38 15 G5
Shepherds Way. TN35 6 E3
Sherwood Clo. TN34 16 C3
Shingle Ct. TN38 10 B2
Shirley Dri. TN37 11 E5
Sidney Little Rd. TN38 10 B6
Silchester Rd. TN38 15 F4
Silvan Clo. TN38 10 C6
Silverhill Av. TN37 11 F5
Silverlands Rd. TN37 15 F1
Smithys Clo. TN37 11 F4
Smugglers Way. TN35 6 E2
South St. TN37 15 G5
South Ter. TN35 3 B1
Southdown Av. TN34 12 D6
Southport Clo. TN38 14 D4
Southwater Rd. TN37 15 G3
Southwood Clo. TN35 15 F2
Sovereign Clo. TN34 12 C5
Springfield Rd. TN38 15 F2
Springfield
    Valley Rd. TN38 15 F3
Springside Walk. TN38 15 F3
Squirrel Clo. TN38 10 C6
Stable Mews. TN34 11 F4
Stainsby St. TN37 15 G4

Stanhope Pl. TN38 15 G5
Stanier Rd. TN34 10 C4
Stanley Rd. TN34 3 A1
Starwell Clo. TN34 16 A2
Station Approach. TN34 3 B2
Station Rd. TN34 3 B2
Stirling Rd. TN34 10 D4
Stockleigh Rd. TN38 15 G4
Stone St. TN34 3 C2
Stonebeach Rise. TN38 10 C2
Stonefield Rd. TN34 3 D2
Stonehouse Dri. TN38 11 E6
Stonelink Clo. TN37 10 C2
Stonestile La. TN35 12 B1
Stream La. TN35 6 F3
Streamside Clo. TN34 11 H6
Strongs Pass. TN35 3 F2
Strood Rd. TN37 15 G1
Summer Hill. TN38 15 E3
Sunningdale Dri. TN38 14 D4
Sussex Rd. TN38 15 E5
*Swaines Pass,
    All Saints St. TN34 3 F2
Swallow Bank. TN38 14 D1
Swan Ter. TN34 3 E2
Swynford Dri. TN34 10 C4
Sycamore Clo. TN38 15 E3
Sydney Clo. TN38 11 E6

Tackleway. TN34 3 F2
Tall Ash Dri. TN37 11 F5
Taylor Clo. TN38 10 C5
Teal Ct. TN38 10 B6
Teddar Ter. TN34 13 E4
Telford Rd. TN38 10 D4
Telham Clo. TN34 12 C4
Tenterden Rise. TN34 16 A2
Terrace Rd. TN37 15 G4
Thanet Way. TN34 16 A3
The Avenue. TN35 6 E2
The Beeches. TN37 10 C3
The Bourne. TN34 3 F2
The Broadway. TN35 13 F6
The Byway. TN34 12 B5
The Cheviots. TN34 12 D5
The Choice. TN38 15 E1
The Cloisters. TN37 15 H4
The Close. TN35 6 B3
The Coppice. TN34 16 B4
The Courtyard. TN34 16 A4
The Crescent. TN34 11 F6
The Croft. TN34 3 E2
The Dene. TN35 12 C4
The Drive. TN38 14 D3
The Fairway. TN38 14 D3
The Finches. TN38 10 D4
The Gables. TN34 11 H6
The Glebe. TN34 16 D3
The Green. TN38 15 F3
The Hawthorns. TN37 10 C2
The Heights. TN38 13 G6
The Hoe. TN37 11 E3
The Kestrels. TN38 10 C4
The Lawn. TN38 15 G5
The Links. TN38 14 D3
The Meadows. TN37 11 F4
The Mount. TN38 15 F5
The Oaks. TN37 11 G4
The Ridge. TN35 11 E2
The Ridge West. TN37 10 C2
The Ridings. TN37 11 F4
The Roundel. TN37 11 F4
The Sedges. TN34 14 C3
The Slides. TN38 10 D6
The Spaldings. TN38 14 D2
The Spinney. TN34 16 A4
The Suttons. TN34 14 D1
The Uplands. TN38 15 F4
The Woodlands. TN34 12 A4
Theaklen Dri. TN38 15 F1
Thomas Brassey
    Clo. TN37 11 E4
Tile Barn Rd. TN38 10 C5
Tilekiln La. TN37 13 G6
Torfield Clo. TN37 3 F1
Tower Rd West. TN38 15 F3
Tower Rd. TN37 15 G3
Towerscroft Av. TN37 11 E4
Trafalgar Clo. TN37 10 C2
*Trafalgar Cotts,
    Tackle Way. TN34 3 F2
Trinity St. TN34 3 B3
Trinity Vs. TN34 3 A3
Truman Dri. TN37 10 C3
Tudor Av. TN38 15 E4
Turnberry Clo. TN38 14 D4
Twyford Cres. TN37 11 E5

Under Cliff. TN38 15 F5
Union St. TN38 15 G5
Upper Broomgrove
    Rd. TN34 16 D2
Upper Church Rd. TN37 10 D4
Upper Clarence Rd. TN37 15 G2
Upper Glen Rd. TN37 10 D4
Upper Maze Hill. TN38 15 F4
Upper Park Rd. TN37 15 G2
Upper South Rd. TN37 15 G2

Vale Rd. TN37 15 G1
Valley Side Rd. TN35 12 D6
Vantage Walk. TN38 15 F2
Vermont Way. TN37 10 C3
Vicarage Rd. TN34 16 C4
Victoria Av. TN35 13 E5
Victoria Rd. TN37 15 H4
View Bank. TN35 17 F3
Villa Rd. TN37 15 H4
Vinehall Clo. TN34 12 C4

Wadhurst Clo. TN37 11 E4
Wainwright Clo. TN38 10 B5
Waites La. TN35 6 E2
Waldegrave St. TN34 3 C1
Waldene Clo. TN34 16 C2
Walton Clo. TN37 11 F4
Warren Clo. TN38 14 C3
Warren Rd. TN35 6 B3
Warrior Gdns. TN37 15 G4
Warrior Sq. TN37 15 G4
Wartling Av. TN38 14 D1
Washington Av. TN37 10 C3
Waterloo Clo. TN37 10 C2
Watermens Clo. TN34 12 B6
Watermill Dri. TN38 10 A4
Waterside Clo. TN35 14 F2
Waterworks Rd. TN34 3 C1
Welbeck Av. TN38 15 E5
Wellington Mws. TN34 3 C2
Wellington Pl. TN34 3 C3
Wellington Rd. TN34 3 C3
Wellington Sq. TN34 3 C2
Wellis Gdns. TN38 15 E3
Wentworth Way. TN38 14 D4
West Hill Rd. TN38 15 E5
West St. TN34 16 D5
West View. TN34 16 D3
Westdean Clo. TN37 11 F3
Westerleigh Clo. TN38 15 E3
Western Rd. TN37 15 G4
Westfield La. TN35 1
Westminster Cres. TN34 12 C5
Whatlington Way. TN38 14 C1
Wheatfield Ct. TN37 11 H3
White Rock. TN34 3 A3
White Rock Gdns. TN34 3 A3
White Rock Rd. TN34 3 A3
Whitefriars Rd. TN34 16 C4
Whittingtons Way. TN34 12 C4
Whittlewood Clo. TN38 14 C1
Whitworth Rd. TN37 11 E2
William Rd. TN38 14 C5
Willingdon Av. TN38 10 D4
Willingdon Clo. TN38 10 D4
Willingdon Way. TN38 10 D4
Willow End. TN34 12 B5
Willowbed Walk. TN34 12 A4
Wilmington Rd. TN34 16 C4
Winchelsea La. TN35 13 F4
Winchelsea Rd. TN34 13 E5
Winding St. TN34 3 E2
Windmill Rd. TN38 15 F1
Windsor Rd. TN37 11 E6
Wingate Clo. TN38 15 E2
Winterbourne Clo. TN34 16 A4
Wishing Tree Rd. TN38 14 D2
Wishing Tree Rd Nth. TN38 10 D5
Wishing Tree
    Rd Nth. TN38 10 D5
Woodbrook Rd. TN34 16 B2
Woodland
    Vale Rd. TN37 15 G3
Woodland Way. TN35 6 G2
Woodlands Way. TN35 11 H3
Woods Pass. TN34 3 F2
Woodspring Dri. TN37 11 E6
Wren Ct. TN38 10 B6
Wrotham Clo. TN34 11 H4
Wykeham Rd. TN34 3 A1
Yew Tree Clo. TN34 11 H3
York Gdns. TN34 3 C3
York Rd. TN34 15 G1